~A BINGO BOOK~

Russia
(and the former Soviet Union)
Bingo Book

COMPLETE BINGO GAME IN A BOOK

I0155212

Saint Basil's Cathedral in Moscow

Written By Rebecca Stark
Educational Books 'n' Bingo

PHOTO CREDITS:
Saint Basil's Cathedral, Red Square, Moscow
Photographer: Ludvig 14
http://commons.wikimedia.org/wiki/File:Moscow_StBasilCathedral_d18.jpg

Educational Books 'n' Bingo

ISBN 978-0-87386-484-8

Printed in the U.S.A.

RUSSIA BINGO DIRECTIONS

INCLUDED:

List of Terms

Templates for Additional Terms and Clues

2 Clues per Term

30 Unique Bingo Cards

Markers

1. **Either cut apart the book or make copies of ALL the sheets. You might want to make an extra copy of the clue sheets to use for introduction and review. Keep the sheets in an envelope for easy reuse.**

2. Cut apart the call cards with terms and clues.

3. Pass out one bingo card per student. There are enough for a class of 30.

4. Pass out markers. You may cut apart the markers included in this book or use any other small items of your choice.

5. Decide whether or not you will require the entire card to be filled. Requiring the entire card to be filled provides a better review. However, if you have a short time to fill, you may prefer to have them do the just the border or some other format. Tell the class before you begin what is required.

6. There are 50 terms. Read the list before you begin. If there are any terms that have not been covered in class, you may want to read to the students the term and clues before you begin.

7. There is a blank space in the middle of each card. You can instruct the students to use it as a free space or you can write in answers to cover terms not included. Of course, in this case you would create your own clues. (Templates provided.)

8. Shuffle the cards and place them in a pile. Two or three clues are provided for each term. If you plan to play the game with the same group more than once, you might want to choose a different clue for each game. If not, you may choose to use more than one clue.

9. Be sure to keep the cards you have used for the present game in a separate pile. When a student calls, "Bingo," he or she will have to verify that the correct answers are on his or her card AND that the markers were placed in response to the proper questions. Pull out the cards that are on the student's card keeping them in the order they were used in the game. Read each clue as it was given and ask the student to identify the correct answer from his or her card.

10. If the student has the correct answers on the card AND has shown that they were marked in response to the *correct questions,* then that student is the winner and the game is over. If the student does not have the correct answers on the card OR he or she marked the answers in response to *the wrong questions,* then the game continues until there is a proper winner.

11. If you want to play again, reshuffle the cards and begin again.

Have fun!

TERMS/NAMES INCLUDED

Alaska	Moscow
Alexander I	Nicholas II
Bolsheviks	Novgorod
Catherine the Great	Odessa
Chernobyl	Anna Pavlova
Anton Chekov	Peristroika
Cold War	Peter I
Crimean War	Peter and Paul
Collectivization	Peterhof
Communism (Communists)	Pogrom
Cuban	Vladimir Putin
Cyrillic	Grigori Rasputin
Duma	Romanov
Five-Year Plan(s)	Saint Petersburg
Yuri Gagarin	Siberia
Glasnost	Soviet Union
Mikhail Gorbachev	Sputnik
Gulag	Joseph Stalin
Hermitage	Pyotr Tchaikovsky
Ivan	Lev Tolstoy
Japanese	Tsar
Nikita Khrushchev	Ukraine
Kremlin	Ural Mountains
Vladimir Lenin	Vladivostok
Karl Marx	Volga

Additional Terms

Choose as many additional terms as you would like and write them in the squares. Repeat each as desired. Cut out the squares and randomly distribute them. Instruct the students to place their square on the center space of their card.

Russia Bingo

Clues for Additional Terms

Write two clues for each of your additional terms.

_____ 1. 2.	_____ 1. 2.
_____ 1. 2.	_____ 1. 2.
_____ 1. 2.	_____ 1. 2.

Alaska 1. Russia is separated from ___ by the Bering Sea. 2. The purchase of ___ in 1867 was often referred to as Seward's Folly until the discovery of gold in the Klondike.	**Alexander I** 1. ___ I was emperor during the Napoleonic Wars. 2. Although ___ sometimes sided with Napoleon, he eventually helped form the coalition that defeated him.
Bolsheviks 1. ___ were members of the wing of the Russian Social-Democratic Workers' Party led by Lenin. 2. The ___ seized control of the government in Russia in October 1917 and became the dominant political power.	**Catherine the Great** 1. ___ ruled from 1762–1796. She was loved by the nobles but not the peasants. 2. ___ was probably responsible for the death of her husband, Peter III.
Chernobyl 1. A catastrophic nuclear accident occurred here in 1986. 2. Located along the banks of the Pripyat River, the ___ Nuclear Power Station consisted of four operating 1,000-megawatt power reactors.	**Anton Chekov** 1. Although a physician, he is best known as a playwright and writer of short stories. 2. Among his most famous works are *The Seagull, The Cherry Orchard,* and *Uncle Vanya.*
Cold War 1. The state of political and military tension between the USA and the USSR from about 1947 to 1991 is known as the ___. 2. The ___ was so named because the two major powers each had weapons that threatened mutual destruction but they never met in direct military combat.	**Crimean War** 1. The ___ was a conflict between the Russian Empire and an alliance of the French, British and Ottoman empires as well as the Kingdom of Sardinia. 2. The Battle of Balaclava was fought on October 25, 1854, during the ___.
Collectivization 1. The goal of ___ was to consolidate individual land and labor into collective farms and state farms. 2. ___ was enforced under Stalin. Its purpose was the formation of collective farms, or *kolkhozy,* and state farms, or *sovkhozy.*	**Communism (Communists)** 1. The goal of ___ was to replace private property and a profit-based economy with public ownership and communal control of the major means of production. 2. ___ supported the revolutionary socialism of Karl Marx.

Russia Bingo

Cuban	**Cyrillic**
1. The ___ Missile Crisis was a 13-day confrontation between the Soviet Union, led by Nikita Khrushchev, and the United States, led by President Kennedy. 2. Nuclear missiles installed near the United States were the central factor in the ___ Missile Crisis of October 1962.	1. The Russian writing system uses a version of the ___ alphabet. 2. The ___ alphabet is used for writing Russian and other Slavic languages.
Duma	**Five-Year Plan(s)**
1. The State ___ was a legislative assembly during the late Russian Empire. 2. Along with the State Council, the ___ made up the imperial Russian legislature from 1906 until its dissolution at the time of the March 1917 Revolution.	1. Stalin's seizure of assets, including farms and factories, as part of his ___ led to inefficient production and famine. 2. Stalin's ___ were disasters, but he forbade negative publicity. He exported food even as rural residents died of starvation.
Yuri Gagarin	**Glasnost**
1. ___ was the first human to journey into outer space and orbit Earth. 2. On April 12, 1961, ___ orbited Earth in the spaceship *Vostok 1*.	1. ___ was a policy of increased openness in government institutions. It allowed for more political discussion. 2. The policies of ___ and *peristroika* were instituted by Mikhail Gorbachev.
Mikhail Gorbachev	**Gulag**
1. ___ instituted the policies of *glasnost* and *peristroika*. 2. ___ was General Secretary of the Communist Party of the Soviet Union from 1985–1991 and its only president from 1990–1991.	1. During the Stalin era, the ___ system served as forced labor camps. 2. The largest ___ camps were in the extreme climatic regions of Siberia and the Far North. They were an important element in the Stalinist system of terror.
Hermitage	**Ivan**
1. Today the ___ is a museum of art and culture in Saint Petersburg. 2. The ___'s Winter Palace is the former state residence of the Russian emperors.	1. ___ IV is known in English as ___ the Terrible, but the term *Grozny* is better translated as "Fearsome." 2. ___ the Terrible was Tsar of All the Russias from 1547 to 1584.

Russia Bingo

Japanese 1. The Russo-___ War was a military conflict after which a victorious Japan forced Russia to abandon its expansionist policy in the Far East. 2. The military conflict called the Russo-___ War took place from 1904–05.	**Nikita Khrushchev** 1. ___ was General Secretary of the Communist Party of the Soviet Union from 1953–1964. 2. ___ came to power after the death of Joseph Stalin. He negotiated with President Kennedy during the Cuban Missile Crisis.
Kremlin 1. The phrase "the ___" usually refers to the one in Moscow and is often used as a metonym* for the government of Russia. 2. A ___ is a major fortified central complex found in historic Russian cities. *metonym: the use of the name of one thing for that of another of which it is is an attribute or with which it is associated	**Vladimir Lenin** 1. In 1917 ___ led what became known as the October Revolution. 2. ___ was leader of the Bolshevik faction of the Russian Social Democratic Labor Party.
Karl Marx 1. This revolutionary, historian and economist published *The Communist Manifesto.* 2. After being exiled to London, he wrote the first volume of *Das Kapital.*	**Moscow** 1. ___ is the capital of Russia. 2. Red Square is the central square of ___. It separates the Kremlin from the historic merchant district.
Nicholas II 1. ___ was the last tsar of the Romanovs. He was married to Alexandra. 2. He and his family were executed on July 17, 1918, by the Bolsheviks.	**Novgorod** 1. The city of ___ lies along the Volkhov River. It was founded in the 9th or 10th century. 2. Among this city's medieval monuments is the St. Sophia Cathedral, built between 1045 and 1050.
Odessa 1. Once the largest city of the Ukraine, today ___ is the third largest after Kiev (Kyiv) and Luhansk. 2. In 1905 the ___ Steps, also known as the Potemkin Steps, were the site of a workers' uprising. Russia Bingo	**Anna Pavlova** 1. ___ was a prima ballerina and the most famous dancer of her time. 2. *The Dying Swan,* which she first performed in 1905, became her signature role. © Barbara M Peller

Peristroika 1. The program instituted in the Soviet Union by Mikhail Gorbachev to restructure Soviet economic and political policy is called ___. 2. ___ is the name of the program instituted in the mid-1980s by Gorbachev. It is the Russian word for "restructuring."	**Peter I** 1. He added "the Great" to his name and was tsar from 1682–1725. 2. Under his rule Russia became a major European power. In 1721 he was given the title of Emperor of All Russia.
Peter and Paul 1. The ___ Fortress was the first structure built in St Petersburg. 2. Peter the Great had this fort built in May 1703 to protect the area from possible attack by the Swedish army and navy.	**Peterhof** 1. ___ comprises a series of palaces and gardens that were laid out on the orders of Peter the Great. 2. The Grand ___ Palace in St. Petersburg is sometimes referred as the "Russian Versailles."
Pogrom 1. The word ___ was first used in English to describe the 19th and 20th-century attacks on Jews in the Russian Empire. 2. ___ is a Yiddish variation of the Russian word meaning "thunder."	**Vladimir Putin** 1. ___ is President of Russia as of the writing of this clue (2013). 2. This Russian intelligence officer and politician served as president and as prime minister.
Grigori Rasputin 1. ___ had a reputation as a mystic and faith healer. He was sometimes called the "mad monk." 2. ___ was a favorite of Alexandra Feodorovna, wife of Nicholas II. He was assassinated in 1916.	**Romanov** 1. The House of ___ was the second and last imperial dynasty to rule over Russia. 2. The House of ___ reigned from 1613 until the 1917 overthrow of the monarchy during the February Revolution.
Saint Petersburg 1. This city on the Neva River was founded by Peter the Great. During its history it was also called Petrograd and Leningrad. 2. From 1713 to 1728 and from 1732 to 1918 ___ was the Imperial capital of Russia. Russia Bingo	**Siberia** 1. This huge region of Russia is sometimes called "the sleeping land." Most of the population lives in the south, along the Trans-Siberian Railway. 2. Lake Baikal in ___ is the deepest freshwater lake in the world.

Soviet Union 1. The ___, or USSR, was a union of many republics with a centralized economy and government. It existed between 1922 and 1991. 2. Russia is by far the largest and most populous of the countries that once formed the ___.	***Sputnik*** 1. ___ was the first artificial Earth satellite. 2. ___ I was launched on October 4, 1957, marking the start of the Space Age.
Joseph Stalin 1.___ purged the party of "enemies of the people," resulting in the execution of thousands and the exile of millions to the gulags during the 1930s. 2. His forced collectivization of agriculture resulted in the starvation and death of millions.	**Pyotr Tchaikovsky** 1. This popular composer's works included symphonies, concertos, operas, ballets, and chamber music. 2. The *1812 Overture, Swan Lake* and *The Nutcracker* are among his most famous works.
Lev Tolstoy 1. His works include the novels *War and Peace* and *Anna Karenina*. 2. Fyodor Dostoyevsky, Anton Chekhov, and ___ were three great Russian novelists.	**Tsar** 1. The term ___ is derived from the Latin word *Caesar,* meaning "Emperor." 2. ___ was the official title for rulers from 1547–1721, but it remained in common usage after that.
Ukraine 1. ___ is the second largest country in what was once the Soviet Union. Kiev (Kyiv) is its capital. 2. Kiev, Luhansk, and Odessa are its three largest cities.	**Ural Mountains** 1. The part of Russia east of the ___ is in Asia. 2. The part of Russia west of the ___ is in Europe. Although about 3/4 of Russia is in Asia, about 78% of the population lives in Europe.
Vladivostok 1. ___ is the main base of the Russian Pacific Fleet and the largest Russian port on the Pacific Ocean. 2. The Trans-Siberian Railway connects ___ to Moscow.	**Volga** 1. The ___ is the longest river in Europe. 2. Moscow is on the ___ River.
Russia Bingo	© **Barbara M Peller**

Russia Bingo

Romanov	Alaska	Bolsheviks	Hermitage	Chernobyl
Mikhail Gorbachev	Alexander I	Ural Mountains	Anna Pavlova	Soviet Union
Ukraine	Odessa		Pogrom	Vladivostok
Tsar	Siberia	Lev Tolstoy	Novgorod	Peter I
Peterhof	Nikita Khrushchev	Five-Year Plan(s)	Joseph Stalin	Karl Marx

Russia Bingo: Card No. 1

Russia Bingo

Tsar	Ukraine	Vladimir Lenin	Saint Petersburg	Nicholas II
Peter I	Yuri Gagarin	Crimean War	Siberia	Peter and Paul
Communism (Communists)	Nikita Khrushchev		Kremlin	Lev Tolstoy
Vladimir Putin	Grigori Rasputin	Odessa	Volga	Chernobyl
Soviet Union	Ural Mountains	Five-Year Plan(s)	Mikhail Gorbachev	Joseph Stalin

Russia Bingo

Nikita Khrushchev	Lev Tolstoy	Yuri Gagarin	Novgorod	Ukraine
Peter I	Alexander I	Collectivization	Alaska	Japanese
Siberia	Ural Mountains		Peter and Paul	Catherine the Great
Odessa	Communism (Communists)	Peterhof	Vladimir Putin	Vladimir Lenin
Joseph Stalin	Cuban	Five-Year Plan(s)	Volga	Nicholas II

Russia Bingo: Card No. 3

Russia Bingo

Odessa	Peter and Paul	Bolsheviks	Cuban	Nicholas II
Peristroika	Cold War	Alaska	Saint Petersburg	Ukraine
Pogrom	Vladimir Putin		Karl Marx	Hermitage
Lev Tolstoy	Alexander I	Ural Mountains	Five-Year Plan(s)	Crimean War
Cyrillic	Soviet Union	Anton Chekov	Joseph Stalin	Vladivostok

Russia Bingo

Soviet Union	Chernobyl	Siberia	Crimean War	Cuban
Peristroika	Lev Tolstoy	Collectivization	Kremlin	Alexander I
Bolsheviks	Vladivostok		Anna Pavlova	Ivan
Karl Marx	Nicholas II	Romanov	Volga	Duma
Yuri Gagarin	Five-Year Plan(s)	Ukraine	Odessa	Pogrom

Russia Bingo

Catherine the Great	Peter and Paul	Vladimir Lenin	Nicholas II	Vladivostok
Novgorod	Siberia	Duma	Alaska	Ukraine
Saint Petersburg	Cyrillic		Cold War	Kremlin
Five-Year Plan(s)	Peterhof	Volga	Anton Chekov	Bolsheviks
Peter I	Crimean War	Romanov	Pogrom	Glasnost

Russia Bingo

Romanov	Peter and Paul	Ivan	Lev Tolstoy	Yuri Gagarin
Peter I	Nicholas II	Nikita Khrushchev	Alexander I	Peristroika
Vladivostok	Hermitage		Kremlin	Cold War
Odessa	Vladimir Putin	Collectivization	Tsar	Communism (Communists)
Five-Year Plan(s)	Cuban	Volga	Anton Chekov	Catherine the Great

Russia Bingo: Card No. 7

Russia Bingo

Pogrom	Peter and Paul	Gulag	Novgorod	Cold War
Peristroika	Bolsheviks	Saint Petersburg	Vladivostok	Crimean War
Glasnost	Cuban		Nicholas II	Chernobyl
Joseph Stalin	Odessa	Tsar	Cyrillic	Vladimir Putin
Ural Mountains	Five-Year Plan(s)	Anton Chekov	Siberia	Peter I

Russia Bingo: Card No. 8

Russia Bingo

Kremlin	Yuri Gagarin	Nikita Khrushchev	Glasnost	Cuban
Cyrillic	Nicholas II	Pogrom	Siberia	Peter and Paul
Japanese	Romanov		Alexander I	Gulag
Duma	Chernobyl	Peterhof	Anna Pavlova	Ivan
Vladimir Putin	Volga	Collectivization	Tsar	Karl Marx

Russia Bingo

Tsar	Novgorod	Cold War	Saint Petersburg	Glasnost
Vladivostok	Crimean War	Alaska	Alexander I	Nicholas II
Cuban	Peter and Paul		Hermitage	Communism (Communists)
Peterhof	Karl Marx	Duma	Volga	Japanese
Collectivization	Peter I	Vladimir Lenin	Soviet Union	Pogrom

Russia Bingo

Catherine the Great	Peter and Paul	Siberia	Duma	Peter I
Gulag	Japanese	Anna Pavlova	Kremlin	Alaska
Peristroika	Nicholas II		Vladimir Lenin	Nikita Khrushchev
Collectivization	Ukraine	Volga	Cuban	Tsar
Cyrillic	Five-Year Plan(s)	Romanov	Anton Chekov	Yuri Gagarin

Russia Bingo

Yuri Gagarin	Chernobyl	Japanese	Novgorod	Kremlin
Nikita Khrushchev	Peter I	Bolsheviks	Anton Chekov	Alexander I
Romanov	Ivan		Vladivostok	Saint Petersburg
Five-Year Plan(s)	Vladimir Putin	Nicholas II	Tsar	Peristroika
Peter and Paul	Gulag	Cuban	Cyrillic	Crimean War

Russia Bingo

Duma	Chernobyl	Catherine the Great	Japanese	Vladivostok
Bolsheviks	Gulag	Nicholas II	Kremlin	Communism (Communists)
Novgorod	Crimean War		Nikita Khrushchev	Ivan
Pogrom	Volga	Cold War	Cuban	Tsar
Five-Year Plan(s)	Karl Marx	Anton Chekov	Romanov	Anna Pavlova

Russia Bingo

Mikhail Gorbachev	Nicholas II	Siberia	Kremlin	Cyrillic
Crimean War	Romanov	Japanese	Alexander I	Peter and Paul
Duma	Hermitage		Vladimir Lenin	Collectivization
Karl Marx	Volga	Cuban	Cold War	Catherine the Great
Five-Year Plan(s)	Saint Petersburg	Communism (Communists)	Peter I	Pogrom

Russia Bingo

Anna Pavlova	Kremlin	Siberia	Yuri Gagarin	Novgorod
Catherine the Great	Vladimir Lenin	Alaska	Bolsheviks	Cyrillic
Vladivostok	Romanov		Ukraine	Peter and Paul
Five-Year Plan(s)	Japanese	Gulag	Volga	Duma
Peter I	Vladimir Putin	Anton Chekov	Glasnost	Nikita Khrushchev

Russia Bingo

Cold War	Japanese	Gulag	Glasnost	Grigori Rasputin
Saint Petersburg	Communism (Communists)	Ivan	Peristroika	Hermitage
Duma	Chernobyl		Vladivostok	Nikita Khrushchev
Odessa	Crimean War	Five-Year Plan(s)	Anna Pavlova	Tsar
Cyrillic	Pyotr Tchaikovsky	Anton Chekov	Vladimir Putin	Peter and Paul

Russia Bingo: Card No. 16

Russia Bingo

Collectivization	*Sputnik*	Moscow	Japanese	Mikhail Gorbachev
Anna Pavlova	Cyrillic	Volga	Hermitage	Ivan
Kremlin	Pogrom		Pyotr Tchaikovsky	Gulag
Karl Marx	Peter I	Tsar	Siberia	Communism (Communists)
Peterhof	Duma	Yuri Gagarin	Novgorod	Chernobyl

Russia Bingo

Glasnost	Cuban	Crimean War	Duma	Saint Petersburg
Peter and Paul	Collectivization	Peterhof	Vladivostok	Cyrillic
Kremlin	Communism (Communists)		Moscow	Bolsheviks
Chernobyl	Alaska	Volga	Tsar	Vladimir Lenin
Pyotr Tchaikovsky	Japanese	Siberia	*Sputnik*	Catherine the Great

Russia Bingo

Vladivostok	Catherine the Great	Japanese	Gulag	Tsar
Anna Pavlova	Novgorod	Peter and Paul	Yuri Gagarin	Hermitage
Sputnik	Cuban		Alexander I	Ukraine
Vladimir Lenin	Pyotr Tchaikovsky	Peterhof	Vladimir Putin	Moscow
Bolsheviks	Grigori Rasputin	Peter I	Pogrom	Anton Chekov

Russia Bingo: Card No. 19

Russia Bingo

Mikhail Gorbachev	*Sputnik*	Novgorod	Japanese	Anton Chekov
Crimean War	Nikita Khrushchev	Peristroika	Peterhof	Saint Petersburg
Chernobyl	Ivan		Odessa	Alaska
Soviet Union	Ural Mountains	Joseph Stalin	Vladimir Putin	Pyotr Tchaikovsky
Lev Tolstoy	Pogrom	Grigori Rasputin	Tsar	Moscow

Russia Bingo: Card No. 20

Russia Bingo

Anna Pavlova	Catherine the Great	Peristroika	Japanese	Soviet Union
Chernobyl	Moscow	Cold War	Gulag	Romanov
Communism (Communists)	Peter I		*Sputnik*	Siberia
Peterhof	Yuri Gagarin	Pyotr Tchaikovsky	Karl Marx	Pogrom
Odessa	Grigori Rasputin	Anton Chekov	Collectivization	Vladimir Putin

Russia Bingo: Card No. 21

Russia Bingo

Glasnost	Vladimir Lenin	Moscow	Bolsheviks	Duma
Saint Petersburg	Novgorod	Ukraine	Gulag	Alexander I
Crimean War	Hermitage		Romanov	Ivan
Pyotr Tchaikovsky	Karl Marx	Vladimir Putin	Alaska	Peristroika
Grigori Rasputin	Collectivization	*Sputnik*	Communism (Communists)	Odessa

Russia Bingo

Cold War	*Sputnik*	Yuri Gagarin	Bolsheviks	Anton Chekov
Catherine the Great	Mikhail Gorbachev	Peter I	Anna Pavlova	Alaska
Vladimir Lenin	Duma		Joseph Stalin	Romanov
Communism (Communists)	Grigori Rasputin	Pyotr Tchaikovsky	Collectivization	Vladimir Putin
Soviet Union	Ural Mountains	Pogrom	Peterhof	Moscow

Russia Bingo

Cold War	Pogrom	Mikhail Gorbachev	*Sputnik*	Gulag
Moscow	Anton Chekov	Peristroika	Saint Petersburg	Romanov
Ivan	Glasnost		Duma	Communism (Communists)
Soviet Union	Joseph Stalin	Pyotr Tchaikovsky	Collectivization	Chernobyl
Lev Tolstoy	Odessa	Grigori Rasputin	Novgorod	Ural Mountains

Russia Bingo

Odessa	Peristroika	*Sputnik*	Siberia	Moscow
Alaska	Chernobyl	Anna Pavlova	Cold War	Alexander I
Karl Marx	Gulag		Joseph Stalin	Pyotr Tchaikovsky
Ukraine	Soviet Union	Ural Mountains	Grigori Rasputin	Hermitage
Anton Chekov	Mikhail Gorbachev	Crimean War	Cyrillic	Lev Tolstoy

Russia Bingo: Card No. 25

Russia Bingo

Moscow	*Sputnik*	Vladimir Lenin	Saint Petersburg	Glasnost
Peterhof	Novgorod	Gulag	Mikhail Gorbachev	Cold War
Karl Marx	Joseph Stalin		Hermitage	Odessa
Collectivization	Bolsheviks	Soviet Union	Grigori Rasputin	Pyotr Tchaikovsky
Ivan	Cyrillic	Siberia	Ural Mountains	Lev Tolstoy

Russia Bingo

Vladimir Lenin	Crimean War	*Sputnik*	Mikhail Gorbachev	Nikita Khrushchev
Soviet Union	Joseph Stalin	Anna Pavlova	Pyotr Tchaikovsky	Alexander I
Volga	Ural Mountains		Grigori Rasputin	Odessa
Glasnost	Catherine the Great	Peristroika	Lev Tolstoy	Alaska
Cyrillic	Hermitage	Moscow	Ukraine	Ivan

Russia Bingo

Vladimir Lenin	Mikhail Gorbachev	Ukraine	*Sputnik*	Cold War
Nikita Khrushchev	Moscow	Joseph Stalin	Saint Petersburg	Hermitage
Ural Mountains	Communism (Communists)		Ivan	Peterhof
Tsar	Glasnost	Peter I	Grigori Rasputin	Pyotr Tchaikovsky
Bolsheviks	Kremlin	Cyrillic	Lev Tolstoy	Soviet Union

Russia Bingo

Moscow	Mikhail Gorbachev	Glasnost	Anna Pavlova	Kremlin
Vladimir Putin	Peterhof	Peristroika	Ivan	Ukraine
Karl Marx	Joseph Stalin		Alexander I	*Sputnik*
Nikita Khrushchev	Soviet Union	Nicholas II	Grigori Rasputin	Pyotr Tchaikovsky
Yuri Gagarin	Gulag	Lev Tolstoy	Catherine the Great	Ural Mountains

Russia Bingo: Card No. 29

Russia Bingo

Cuban	*Sputnik*	Saint Petersburg	Kremlin	Pyotr Tchaikovsky
Alaska	Mikhail Gorbachev	Vladimir Lenin	Hermitage	Alexander I
Karl Marx	Duma		Ivan	Peristroika
Lev Tolstoy	Catherine the Great	Bolsheviks	Grigori Rasputin	Joseph Stalin
Soviet Union	Vladivostok	Ural Mountains	Moscow	Ukraine

www.ingramcontent.com/pod-product-compliance
Lightning Source LLC
LaVergne TN
LVHW061338060426
835511LV00014B/2000